# Drew and the Crew

**Pam Scheunemann**

Consulting Editor, Diane Craig, M.A./Reading Specialist

**ABDO**
Publishing Company

Published by ABDO Publishing Company, 4940 Viking Drive, Edina, Minnesota 55435.

Credits
Edited by: Pam Price
Curriculum Coordinator: Nancy Tuminelly
Cover and Interior Design and Production: Mighty Media
Photo Credits: AbleStock, Tracy Kompelien, Photodisc, Wewerka Photography

Library of Congress Cataloging-in-Publication Data

Scheunemann, Pam, 1955-
    Drew and the crew / Pam Scheunemann.
        p. cm. -- (First rhymes)
    Includes index.
    ISBN 1-59679-473-9 (hardcover)
    ISBN 1-59679-474-7 (paperback)
        1. English language--Rhyme--Juvenile literature. I. Title. II. Series.
PE1517.S424 2005
808.1--dc22

                                                                    2005048552

SandCastle™ books are created by a professional team of educators, reading specialists, and content developers around five essential components that include phonemic awareness, phonics, vocabulary, text comprehension, and fluency. All books are written, reviewed, and leveled for guided reading and early intervention reading, and designed for use in shared, guided, and independent reading and writing activities to support a balanced approach to literacy instruction.

## Let Us Know

After reading the book, SandCastle would like you to tell us your stories about reading. What is your favorite page? Was there something hard that you needed help with? Share the ups and downs of learning to read. We want to hear from you! To get posted on the ABDO Publishing Company Web site, send us e-mail at:

**sandcastle@abdopub.com**

**SandCastle Level: Beginning**

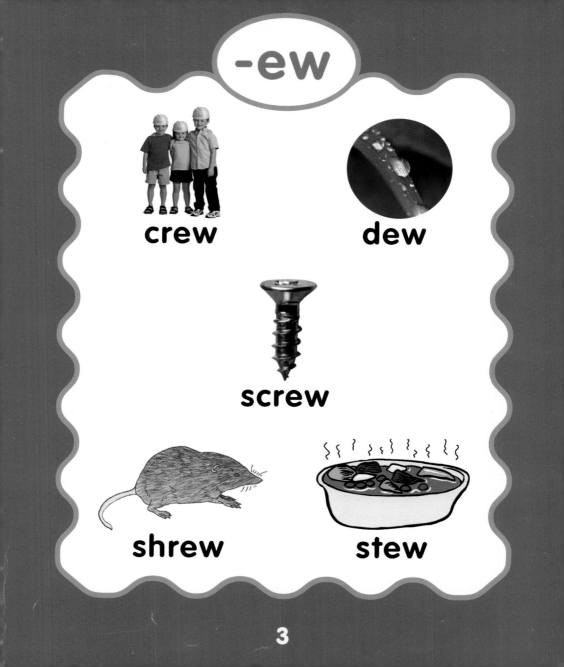

# -ew

crew

dew

screw

shrew

stew

3

They are a  .

This is  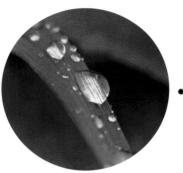.

This is a 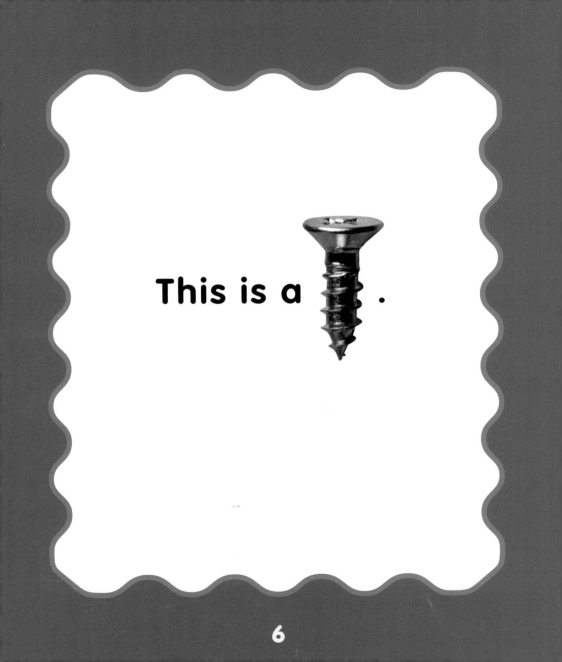 .

Here is a  .

This is  .

They work on a crew.

There is dew
on the leaf.

# The screw is little.

# Drew and the Crew

The screw is little.

# The shrew has fur.

# The stew is hot.

# Drew and the Crew

Drew was part
of a crew.

Drew and the crew
had a very big screw.

Drew blew the dew
from the big screw.

Drew and the crew
flew on the screw
to see a shrew.

Drew and the crew
landed the big screw
at the home
of the shrew.

"Hey, Drew,"
said the shrew,
"do you and the crew
want some stew?"

# About SandCastle™

A professional team of educators, reading specialists, and content developers created the SandCastle™ series to support young readers as they develop reading skills and strategies and increase their general knowledge. The SandCastle™ series has four levels that correspond to early literacy development in young children. The levels are provided to help teachers and parents select the appropriate books for young readers.

**Emerging Readers**
(no flags)

**Beginning Readers**
(1 flag)

**Transitional Readers**
(2 flags)

**Fluent Readers**
(3 flags)

These levels are meant only as a guide. All levels are subject to change.

**ABDO**
**Publishing Company**

To see a complete list of SandCastle™ books and other nonfiction titles from ABDO Publishing Company, visit **www.abdopub.com** or contact us at:
4940 Viking Drive, Edina, Minnesota 55435 • 1-800-800-1312 • fax: 1-952-831-1632

LAWRENCE BRANCH